Sloths

Sloths

A Carolrhoda Nature Watch Book

by Melissa Stewart

Carolrhoda Books, Inc. / Minneapolis

CONTENTS

For Gerard, who is certainly no sloth

Copyright © 2005 by Melissa Stewart

Carolrhoda Books, Inc.
A division of Lerner Publishing Group
241 First Avenue North
Minneapolis, MN 55401 U.S.A.

Website address: www.lernerbooks.com

Library of Congress Cataloging-in-Publication Data

Stewart, Melissa.
    Sloths / Melissa Stewart
      p.   cm. — (A Carolrhoda nature watch book)
    Includes index.
    Summary:
    ISBN: 1–57505–577–5 (pbk. : alk. paper)
    The life cycles of the two-toed and three-toed sloths, their habitat and habits, and how they are being affected by loss of rain forest. I. Title. II. Series
    QL638.S2 H54 2005
    597.5'6—dc21   00–008382

Manufactured in the United States of America
1 2 3 4 5 6 – JR – 10 09 08 07 06 05

Left: *Sloths, like this Hoffman's two-toed sloth, spend most of their lives hanging upside down in tropical forest trees.*
Right: *The rain forests of Costa Rica are home to several kinds of sloths.*

SLOTHS THROUGH TIME

Deep in a Central American rain forest, monkeys spend their days chattering as they leap from branch to branch. Above them, brightly colored birds call out to one another as they fly among the treetops. Far below, on the forest floor, butterflies flit above the leaf litter. The woodland is alive with sound and activity. But one rain forest animal remains silent and still. It is the sloth. All day and most of the night, this shaggy-coated creature hardly moves at all. It hangs upside down and does its best to blend in with its surroundings.

The word *sloth* means "laziness," so it's a good name for the slowest **mammal** in the world. A mammal is an animal that has a backbone, or spine, and feeds its young mother's milk. Most mammals also have four legs and hairy bodies. Dogs, cats, mice, horses, and elephants are all mammals, and so are humans.

The first mammals lived on Earth about 230 million years ago. But for millions of years, they were a relatively minor group of animals. During all that time, the planet was ruled by dinosaurs and their reptile relatives.

About 65 million years ago, all that suddenly changed when a giant space rock crashed into Earth. The force of the impact thrust tons of ash and dust into the air, blocking out the Sun's bright, warming rays for many months.

Without sunlight, most of Earth's plants and animals died. But a few small mammals were among the animals that managed to survive. These hardy creatures evolved into the more than 4,500 **species,** or kinds, of mammals alive today.

About 5 million years after the space rock struck our planet, a new group of mammals developed in what is present-day South America. They had simple, peglike teeth and small brains and unusual or extra bones in their spines. These cat-sized creatures were the ancestors of all modern anteaters, armadillos, and sloths. They spent most of their time in trees and ate only plants.

For millions of years, South America was an isolated island continent with plenty of food and few **predators,** animals that kill and eat other animals. Under these conditions, early anteaters, armadillos, and sloths thrived. About 35 million years ago, some species began to live on the ground. No longer confined to trees, the animals quickly increased in size and spread over a wider range. At their height, several dozen species of tree and ground sloths lived on Earth.

Giant ground sloths lived in North and South America 35 million years ago.

This full-size model of a giant ground sloth is taller than some of the trees.

The largest ground sloths to ever live were as big as elephants. These giant sloths wandered the ancient grasslands of South America, browsing on the scattered trees and shrubs. Some scientists believe these giant sloths may have also eaten small animals that they killed with their sharp claws, which were 7 inches (20 cm) long.

During the Ice Age, a time period that was from 1.8 million years ago to about 12,000 years ago, many giant ground sloths crossed a land bridge that formed between North and South America. Four ox-sized sloth species migrated as far north as the southern United States. These huge creatures all died out about 10,000 years ago.

But five species of their smaller tree-dwelling relatives can still be found in the tropical forests of Central and South America.

Scientists divide the five species of modern sloths into two groups, based on the number of toes on their front feet—the two-toed sloths and the three-toed sloths.

The two-toed sloths are the Linné's sloth and the Hoffman's sloth. The three-toed species are the pale-faced, the brown-throated, and the maned sloth.

The brown-throated sloth has three toes on both its front and back feet.

Hoffman's two-toed sloth has two toes on its front feet and three toes on its back feet.

The true two-toed sloth, also known as Linné's two-toed sloth, lives in the forests of northern South America. It has coarse, bristly brownish-gray fur and lives alone or in small groups.

The Hoffman's sloth is very similar to the true two-toed sloth, but it has a much larger range. It can be found as far north as Nicaragua, through Central America, and as far south as Peru and Brazil.

Although both species have two toes on their front feet, the Hoffman's sloth has three toes on its back feet, while the true two-toed sloth has only two.

Three-toed sloths look very similar to their two-toed cousins. As adults, they are 16 to 28 inches (41–71 cm) long and usually weigh no more than 12 pounds (5.4 kg). Unlike two-toed sloths, three-toed sloths have a small tail. Three-toed sloths have more **vertebrae** (VER-tuh-bray), or bones in their spines, than two-toed sloths. As a result, three-toed sloths can turn their heads farther to the right and left than their relatives. Some three-toed sloths can turn their heads almost all the way around. This allows them to look down at the forest floor while they are hanging upside down.

Three-toed sloths have small tails and can turn their heads nearly all the way around.

Ranges of the Two-toed and Three-toed Sloths

CENTRAL AMERICA

ATLANTIC OCEAN

GUATEMALA
EL SALVADOR
HONDURAS
NICARAGUA
COSTA RICA
PANAMA

VENEZUELA

GUYANA
SURINAM
FRENCH GUIANA

COLOMBIA

EQUADOR

SOUTH AMERICA

PACIFIC OCEAN

PERU

BOLIVIA

BRAZIL

N

CHILE

PARAGUAY

ARGENTINA

The true three-toed sloth, also known as the pale-faced three-toed sloth, lives in southern Central America to northeast Argentina. It has a round, yellowish face and a long neck. Its front legs are nearly twice as long as its back legs.

The brown-throated three-toed sloth can be found in the tropical forests of Guatemala and Honduras. It has a flat face with dark brown stripes near its eyes. Like other sloths, it spends many hours each day hanging upside down. But it also spends some time sitting in the forks of trees where two branches meet.

The maned sloth has a long black mane that runs down its neck to the middle of its back. It is the rarest species of sloth and lives only in eastern Brazil.

The maned sloth lives in eastern Brazil.

Tropical forest are home to enormous variety of plants and animals.

AT HOME IN THE TROPICAL FOREST

Sloths are among the most common mammals in the tropical rain forests and tropical **deciduous** (dih-SIH-juh-wahs) forests of Central and South America. These woodlands, which form a band around the equator 3,000 miles (4,800 km) wide, are warm all year long. They receive up to 360 inches (910 cm) of rain annually and about 12 hours of sunlight every day.

Because growing conditions are so good, tropical forests contain an incredible variety of plants and animals. Even though tropical forests cover only 7 percent of Earth's surface, they are home to more than half of all known species of plants and animals.

In tropical rain forests, all the trees are evergreens. Like the pine and spruce trees that grow in North America, tropical rain forest trees lose their leaves a few at a time, rather than all at once. As a result, very little sunlight trickles through the leafy **canopy** to the forest floor. Although the canopy and **understory** of a rain forest are lush and green, few plants can survive on the shady forest floor.

In tropical deciduous forests, the trees are not green throughout the year. Like the oaks and maples that grow in North America, they lose all their leaves at once. But instead of falling in the autumn, the leaves of tropical deciduous trees drop at the start of the dry season. When wet season rains return to these woodlands, the trees spring back to life, and an explosion of greenery spreads across the land. During the dry season, plenty of light can reach the forest floor. As a result, a wide variety of vines, small plants, and shrubs thrive, giving tropical deciduous forests a dense, junglelike appearance.

Layers of a Tropical Forest

Canopy

Understory

Forest Floor

In a tropical rainforest, trees in the canopy and understory keep their leaves all year round, so the forest floor is always in shade.

While some creatures prefer to live in either tropical rain forests or tropical deciduous forests, sloths have many adaptations that make them successful in both **habitats.** They have no trouble finding food or avoiding tropical predators, and they are perfectly suited to the hot, humid weather. Sloths are true survivors.

Right side up or upside down sloths are at home in the hot, humid weather of tropical forests.

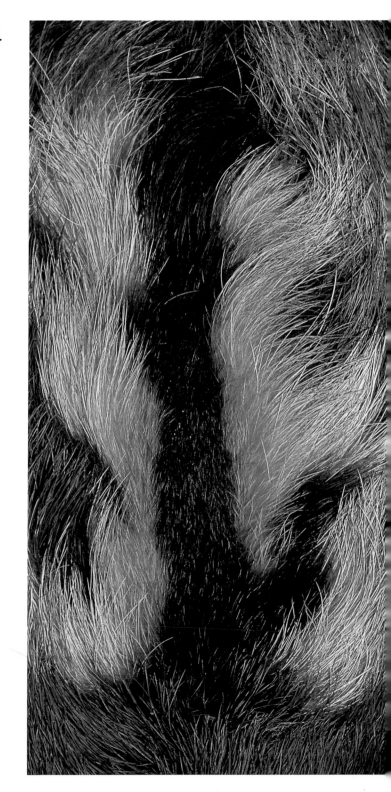

During the day, sloths sleep dangling upside down from tree limbs. For a few early evening or night hours, they move hand over hand through the trees as they search for tasty leaves, buds, fruits, and twigs. Sloths move slowly and carefully, so they hardly ever fall. These amazing animals even mate and give birth while suspended from their long, curved claws.

Because sloths have such an unusual upside-down lifestyle, many of their internal organs are in different positions from other mammals. Their stiff, wiry hair grows differently than the coats of other animals do. It grows from the belly toward the back, instead of from the back to the belly, allowing rainwater to run off. Below this tough top layer, a dense downy layer of fur provides additional protection from deadly enemies as well as pesky insects.

Sloths weigh less than other mammals their size, so they have no trouble climbing onto thin branches high in the tropical forest canopy. They weigh relatively little because they have only about half as much muscle mass as other similar-sized mammals. Any athlete knows that maintaining muscles takes a great deal of food energy. Since sloths don't have as much muscle as other mammals, they don't need to eat as much food.

The lightweight sloth can climb out onto thin branches to feed.

Both two- and three-toed sloths have lower body temperatures than most mammals, so they eat less than other mammals their size.

A sloth can also survive on smaller amounts of food because it has a lower body temperature than other mammals. All mammals, including humans, are **warm-blooded** creatures. This means their body temperature stays relatively steady no matter how warm or cold it is.

A person's body temperature is usually about 98.6°F (37°C). Healthy dogs, cats, horses, sheep, rabbits, pigs, and cows all have body temperatures between 100 and 103°F (38–39°C). A sloth's body temperature is much lower—usually around 93°F (34°C).

In addition, a sloth's body temperature changes slightly as the temperature of its surroundings changes. Like snakes, frogs, and other **cold-blooded** animals, a sloth's body temperature is highest on warm, sunny days and lowest at night and on rainy days. Sometimes a sloth sunbathes in the morning to warm its body up. Then, during the hottest part of the day, the sloth hides in the shade so it will not overheat. During the course of a normal day, a sloth's body temperature may fluctuate by as much as 10°F (6°C). If the body temperature of a person, a dog, or a cow rose or fell just 5°F (3°C), it would probably die.

When a sloth is cold, its entire body slows down. It moves even less than usual, and its heartbeat and breathing slow. When the animal's body is working at a slower pace, it uses less energy and requires less food. Because a cold sloth eats so little, it usually cannot raise its body temperature on its own. It must wait for the sun's warm rays.

This Hoffman's two-toed sloth is warming up in the sun. It will move to the shade in the hottest parts of the day.

A sloths's back legs are so weak that it can't walk when it is on the ground. This three-toed sloth is using its claws to pull itself along.

Even though a sloth has less overall muscle mass than other animals, its shoulder, neck, and front leg muscles are quite strong. But its back legs are so weak that the animal cannot walk. When a sloth is on the ground, it must lie on its stomach and reach ahead for a toehold. Then it uses its long claws to slowly drag its body forward.

Luckily, sloths spend very little time on the ground. They can get just about everything they need high above the forest floor. The leafy understory and canopy provide sloths with plenty of food and water. The water comes from eating juicy leaves and licking up drops of morning dew.

A brown-throated three-toed sloth hangs by its back legs while it reaches for a tasty leaf.

FOOD FACTS

At feeding time, a sloth grabs leaves with its flexible feet or tears them with its hard, tough lips. Then it grinds the food with the large peglike teeth on the sides of its mouth. A sloth's teeth wear down quickly, so it's a good thing they never stop growing.

A sloth digests its food just as it does everything else—very slowly. People usually digest food in about 1 day. A sloth may take as long as 1 month.

Special **bacteria** live inside a sloth's stomach and intestines. As soon as a sloth swallows a mouthful of pulverized (chewed-up) plants, these bacteria begin breaking down the food. It will take many hours for the bacteria to digest this tough plant material. Only then can the sloth absorb the **nutrients** it needs to live and grow.

Most sloths eat only a few kinds of trees. To locate its favorite foods in the dark, a sloth relies on its keen senses of smell and touch. Each individual's food preferences are determined by the bacteria living in its gut. These bacteria are passed on to a young sloth when its mother shares her food with her baby. Because each animal has such a specific diet, sloths rarely compete for food.

Each sloth eats only a few kinds of leaves. This maned sloth has found one of the kind that it likes.

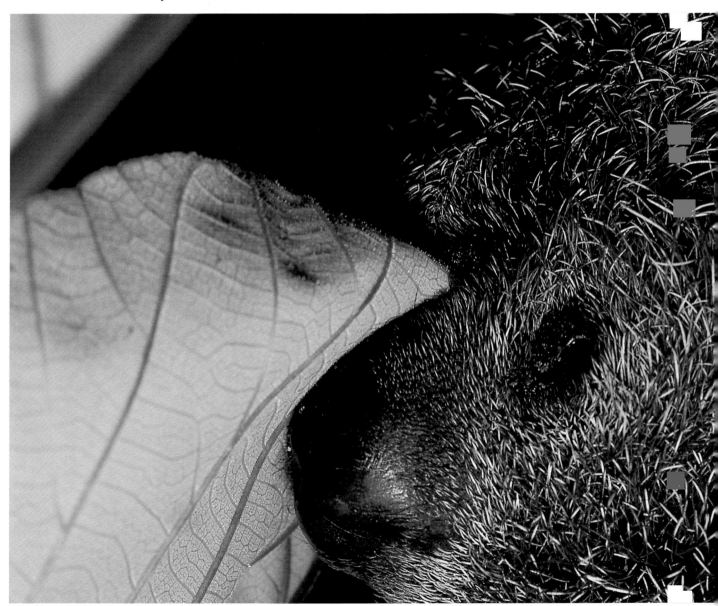

Three-toed sloths usually feed in the late afternoon and early evening. They have a strict diet of leaves, buds, and tender twigs. They spend their entire lives in a relatively small area of forest and move very little as they **forage**, or look for food.

Above: *The brown-throated, like all three-toed sloths, feeds in the late afternoon or early evening.*
Left: *Two-toed sloths, like this Hoffman's, feed only at night.*

During rainy season, heavy rain falls in the tropical forests every afternoon.

Two-toed sloths feed only at night, but they move around a bit more than their three-toed cousins. They rarely stay in the same tree for more than 1 day. Two-toed sloths eat mostly leaves and twigs, but they also dine on fruits and an occasional insect or bird's egg.

During the rainy season in the tropical forests, each day begins with clear skies and a few cottony clouds. But in the afternoon, the weather changes dramatically. The wind picks up, and a thick wall of clouds rolls across the darkening sky. In the distance, lightning flashes and thunder booms. A few moments later, sheets of rain drench the land. Lightning bolts zigzag to the ground. Thunder crackles and crashes.

During dry season, sloths must descend from the trees to deposit their wastes onto the ground.

All the noise and falling water provides the perfect opportunity for sloths to let out their waste materials without attracting the attention of hungry predators. During the dry season, getting rid of wastes is a bit more difficult. When no rain falls, a sloth can store up its waste materials for about 1 week. Then it slowly descends to the ground, digs a hole, and deposits up to 2 pounds (1 kg) of dung. That's a lot of waste for an animal that may weigh only 10 pounds (5 kg)! After filling in the hole, the sloth climbs back up the tree.

A sloth deposited these wastes at the base of the tree.

This entire process may take more than an hour. It requires a lot of precious energy and may attract the attention of hungry predators. Why does a sloth go to so much trouble? No one knows for sure. Some scientists think that burying the dung may help fertilize the trees that sloths depend on for food. Others believe burying dung may make it more difficult for predators on the ground to track sloths. While scientists may not agree on why sloths engage in such a dangerous behavior, the benefits to other creatures are more obvious.

Each time a sloth deposits dung, dozens of sloth moths living in its furry coat lay their eggs on the droppings. After the eggs hatch, the young caterpillars feed on nutrients in the dung. As the caterpillars grow, they **molt,** or shed their outer covering, several times. Eventually, they enter a resting stage called a **pupa** before transforming into a winged adult. The moths then fly up into the trees in search of another sloth to live on.

The moths hovering around
this mother and baby sloth
will lay their eggs on her droppings.

Algae grows on the hair of sloths during rainy season, giving them a greenish tinge.

Moths are far from the only creatures found in a sloth's dense fur. Hundreds of beetles, mites, and ticks spend their entire lives hanging out with sloths. While some of these tiny residents feed directly on the sloth, others munch on slimy green **algae** (AL-jee) that grow on the animal's fur during the rainy season.

Each of the long, coarse hairs that makes up a sloth's shaggy coat has a deep groove, providing the perfect spot for a colony of algae to live and grow. The algae give the sloth's coat a greenish tinge, which helps the animal blend into its forest surroundings. From time to time, the algae also provides a quick, nutritious meal. The sloth just leans over and licks some of the green slime off its hair.

This three-toed sloth mother can lick up the algae when she needs a quick meal.

If a hungry predator looked up, it probably wouldn't even notice this sleeping sloth.

AVOIDING ENEMIES

Sloths have many enemies, but most of the time, they manage to avoid attracting attention. As long as an algae-coated sloth remains perfectly quiet and still, it is nearly impossible to detect. For most of the day, a sloth sleeps curled up in a tight ball in a tree fork or hangs from a tree branch with all four legs close together and its head tucked between its front legs. Any predator that notices a sleeping sloth is likely to think it is part of a tree or mistake it for a termite nest.

Occasionally, a harpy eagle's sharp eyes spot a sleeping sloth. Although the bird usually hunts small monkeys, opossums, and other medium-sized mammals, it will not pass up a chance to dine on tasty sloth meat.

Despite the harpy eagle's huge size, it has relatively small wings, allowing it to navigate through dense tropical forest areas. As the bird pursues a quick little monkey, it can weave through trees and shrubs at more than 50 miles (80 km) per hour. But such speed is not necessary to catch a sluggish sloth.

When a hungry harpy eagle spots a sloth, it lunges toward the hanging animal with its huge, sharp talons, or claws. But before the bird can snatch the **prey**, it's in for quite a fight. Sloths have excellent hearing. At the first sign of attack, the sloth shakes itself awake. It hisses at its enemy, and lashes out with its own sharp claws. If the eagle gets close enough, the sloth may try to bite it.

Before this harpy eagle can kill a sloth, it will have to put up quite a fight.

A sloth traveling along the ground is an easy target for a jaguar.

Because the eagle must try to dislodge the sloth while flapping its wings to stay airborne, the sloth has an important advantage. The mammal's heavy fur and thick, tough skin also offer some protection against the hungry hunter's attack. In addition, the sloth's chest cavity is surrounded by wide, tightly spaced ribs that protect the animal's delicate internal organs. While the ripping power of the harpy eagle's talons will probably wound the sloth severely, the bird may not be able to kill the sloth.

Although a sloth is relatively safe in the forest's understory, its weak back legs make it almost helpless on the ground. As a result, sloths rarely descend to the forest floor. When they deposit dung, they usually travel only a short distance from the tree they have just climbed down. But sometimes, a sloth must cross a wide area of land. If it wants to feed on a tree that it cannot reach by swinging from branch to branch, it has no choice but to clamber down to the forest floor and slowly drag itself across the ground. This risky move makes the sloth an easy target for **ocelots** and **jaguars**.

Like sloths, ocelots and jaguars are **nocturnal** animals. They sleep for most of the day and hunt at night. Their large eyes help them see well in dim light. These wildcats also use their keen senses of smell and hearing to find prey.

An ocelot's tawny yellow fur is covered with dark spots and rings, making it difficult to detect as it rests in the trees or creeps along the forest floor. When an ocelot spots a sloth on the ground, it pounces on the helpless animal and plunges its sharp teeth into the sloth's neck. This kills the sloth instantly.

Most of the time, an ocelot will eat its kill on the spot, but if it is raising a litter of cubs, the ocelot will drag the meal back to its den. Besides sloths, ocelots eat fish, snakes, lizards, turtles, frogs, birds, and small mammals.

A jaguar looks similar to an ocelot, but it is much bigger. An ocelot isn't much larger than a house cat, but an adult male jaguar may be 6 feet (2 m) long and weigh as much as 250 pounds (110 kg).

The ocelot's yellow, spotted coat makes it hard to see in the forest.

As a jaguar stalks prey, it uses its razor-sharp claws to scramble up trees or it silently creeps along the ground on its soft, padded paws. A jaguar can chase its prey with speed and agility, but when it spots a sloth on the ground, the hunter simply grabs the animal by the neck and shakes it savagely. A jaguar can quickly crush the skull of a sloth with its powerful jaws. While a jaguar can subdue prey as large as deer, wild pigs, and alligators, it is not a picky eater. It will eat just about anything that crosses its path.

A jaguar will climb trees to stalk prey. It can crush a sloth's skull with its powerful jaws.

This brown-throated sloth shows its swimming skills in crossing a river in Panama.

Sloths are good swimmers, so although they are at great risk on land, they have a much better chance of survival in the water. Since their back legs are so weak, they use a kind of breaststroke to move through the water. Their tough skin protects sloths from the sharp teeth of piranhas and other meat-eating fish, but the water is far from a safe place. Both ocelots and jaguars are excellent swimmers too and often catch prey in the water. A swimming sloth must also beware of anacondas—huge snakes that kill prey by coiling their large, powerful bodies around their victim and squeezing until the animal drowns or stops breathing.

A large adult anaconda may be 20 feet (6 m) long and weigh as much as 230 pounds (100 kg). These snakes blend in well with their surroundings and are almost impossible to detect—until it is too late. Anacondas often lie in wait near a river and attack animals when they come for a drink, but these stealthy hunters also attack swimming animals from below.

Even though sloths face many dangers in their tropical forest home, they continue to be among the most common mammals living there. Large numbers of sloths manage to survive by avoiding their enemies and fighting fiercely when they have to. The sloth population also remains healthy because sloth mothers devote a lot of time and energy to raising their young.

The huge anaconda can kill a sloth by coiling around it and squeezing, just as it is doing to an iguana (i-GWAN-uh)—a tropical lizard—in this photo.

Most sloths live alone except at mating time.

RAISING A FAMILY

Most sloths are solitary creatures. Male sloths spend nearly all their time alone. So do female three-toed sloths. But small groups of two-toed females sometimes live together. Adult males and females come together only when it is time to mate.

When a female is ready to mate, she lets out a high-pitched scream in the middle of the night. Within a few hours, any males in the area are slowly moving toward the female. If two males arrive at the same time, they each grasp a tree branch with their back legs and swing their front legs at one another. The males continue their upside-down wrestling match until one gives up and leaves. Although male sloths may injure one another with their sharp claws, the wounds usually aren't severe.

During the next few hours, the victorious male mates with the female several times. Then he leaves, and the female is on her own.

Most females give birth to one tiny baby after 6 months, but Hoffman's sloths are pregnant for almost 1 year. A newborn sloth is about 10 inches (25 cm) long and weighs about 12 ounces (340 g).

For the next 5 to 6 weeks, the helpless baby clings tightly to the shaggy hair on its mother's belly. If the youngster loses its grip and falls, the mother will usually not rescue her little one. She knows that the baby's cries will quickly attract the attention of hungry predators.

This baby three-toed sloth clings tightly to its mother.

This three-toed sloth is sharing a leaf with its two-month old baby.

At first, the baby feeds only on its mother's rich, nutritious milk. But later, it begins to nibble on leaves, learning which plants are good to eat and which are not. While the youngster clings to its mother, it will eat whatever leaves it can reach. It is during this period that the young sloth learns to prefer certain species of trees.

As the youngster grows, it spends less time with its mother and more time on its own. It learns to hang upside down by itself and stops drinking mother's milk. When the little sloth is ready to be on its own, its mother leaves it and moves to another part of her home range. Some sloth species can survive on their own when they are just 6 months old, but others stay with their mothers for up to 2 years.

Female sloths are ready to start families of their own when they are about 3 years old, but males usually do not begin to mate until they are 4 or 5 years old. In their tropical forest home, sloths usually live about 12 years, but a few may live to be 20 years old. This means that an average female sloth will have about nine babies in her lifetime.

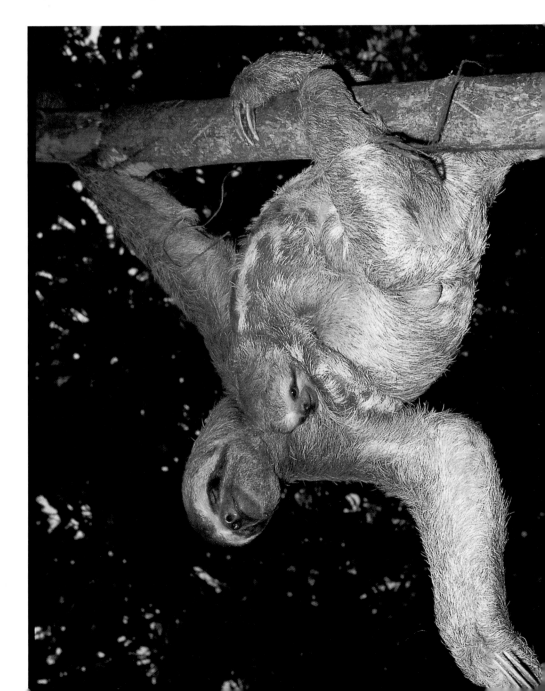

The young three-toed sloth holds on tight to its mother as she climbs through the trees.

This brown-throated three-toed sloth is just one of many kinds of sloths living successfully in tropical forest habitats.

CAN SLOTHS SURVIVE?

Although tree sloths have many enemies, they have managed to survive on Earth for millions of years. Because they spend most of their time in the trees and move very little during the day, most predators do not notice them. Even when sloths are attacked, they can use their sharp claws to fight back.

Recently, however, a new enemy has begun to threaten sloths. Although humans rarely hunt sloths, people are killing hundreds, possibly even thousands, of these animals each year. As people cut down tropical forests for timber or burn them so the land can be used for farming, sloths and many other creatures are losing their homes.

In the last 30 years, more than 40 percent of the world's tropical forests have been destroyed. Each year another 27 million acres (11 million hectares) are leveled. Experts predict that if the destruction continues at this rate, tropical forests will be gone in 50 years. While some tropical forest creatures may be able to survive in other habitats or in zoos, sloths are very fussy about their food and their surroundings. If the tropical forests of Central and South America disappear, sloths will vanish too.

Despite the rate of tropical forest destruction, most sloth populations are thriving. Only the maned sloth is currently considered an **endangered species**. It is **extinct,** gone forever, in most of its natural range because huge areas of Brazilian rain forest have been cut down or burned.

People are beginning to understand the value of tropical forests and the wildlife in them. Many groups are working hard to protect and preserve these unique environments. This is good news for sloths and all the other creatures that share their tropical forest habitats.

If their forests are protected from logging and burning, sloths will survive long into the future.

GLOSSARY

algae: tiny organisms that often grow as part of a large colony and are neither plants nor animals

bacteria: one-celled, living creatures that sometimes cause disease. One kind helps sloths digest their food.

canopy: the top layer of a tropical forest

cold blooded: unable to maintain a constant body temperature

deciduous: losing all leaves at a certain time of year, rather than a few leaves at a time

endangered species: an animal in danger of dying out

extinct: having disappeared from Earth forever

forage: search for food

habitats: the areas where a particular group of animals or plants naturally lives, grows, and reproduces

jaguars: large cats weighing up to 250 pounds (110 kg) that live in the tropical rain forest

mammal: an animal that has a backbone and fur and feeds its young mother's milk

molt: to shed or lose feathers, skin, or other outer covering

nocturnal: most active at night

nutrients: substances, especially in food, that are needed for healthy growth

ocelots: predators of the cat family that live in tropical forests

predators: animals that hunt and kill other animals for food

prey: animals that are killed and eaten by other animals

pupa: the resting stage of insect metamorphosis during which a larva transforms itself into an adult

species: a group of organisms that share certain characteristics and can mate and produce healthy young

understory: the middle layer of a tropical forest

vertebrae: the bones in the spine

warm blooded: maintaining a nearly constant body temperature

INDEX

ABOUT THE AUTHOR

Melissa Stewart has always been fascinated by the natural world and is a careful observer. Before becoming a full-time writer, she earned a bachelor's degree in biology from Union College and a master's degree in science and environmental journalism from New York University. She then spent a decade working as a science editor.

Stewart has written more than thirty critically acclaimed children's books about animals, ecosystems, earth science, and space science. She has also contributed articles to a variety of magazines for adults and children, such as *Science World, Odyssey, National Geographic World, Natural New England, American Forests,* and *American Heritage of Invention and Technology.* She lives in Northborough, Massachusetts.

PHOTO ACKNOWLEDGMENTS

Photographs are reproduced through the courtesy of: © Kevin Schafer, pp. 2, 7, 12, 15, 18 (right), 19, 20, 25, 26 (bottom), 28, 40, 45; © Carrol Henderson, pp. 4–5, 10, 16, 24, 29, 30, 32, 44; © Art Wolfe, pp. 6, 11, 41; © American Museum of History Library, pp. 8–9; © Jany Sauvanet/Photo Researchers Inc., pp. 13, 18 (left); © Dan Guravid/Photo Researchers Inc., pp. 21, 23, 42; © Gregory G. Dimijian/Photo Researchers Inc., p. 22; © Larry Kimball/Visuals Unlimited, p. 26 (top); © Jacques Jangoux/Visuals Unlimited, p. 27; © Richard Thom/ Visuals Unlimited, p. 31; © David M. Schleser/Nature's Images Inc./Photo Researchers Inc., pp. 33, 43; © Ken Lucas/Visuals Unlimited, p. 34; © Joe McDonald/Visuals Unlimited, p. 35; © Patrick Spence/Visuals Unlimited, p. 36; © Tom Bakerfield/CORBIS, p. 37; © Michael and Patricia Fogden/CORBIS, p. 38; © Francois Gonier/Photo Researchers Inc., p. 39.

Front cover: © Kevin Schafer.